A Great Idea

HDTV: High Definition Television

by Kris Hirschmann

NORWOODHOUSE PRESS

Norwood House Press
P.O. Box 316598
Chicago, Illinois 60631

For information regarding Norwood House Press, please visit our Web site at:

www.norwoodhousepress.com or call 866-565-2900.

LIBRARY OF CONGRESS CATALOGING-IN-PUBLICATION DATA

Hirschmann, Kris, 1967-
  HDTV : high definition television / Kris Hirschmann.
    p. cm. — (A great idea)
  Includes bibliographical references and index.
  Summary: "Chronicles the development and availability of high-definition televisions (HDTVs). Topics include explanations of how HDTV works, difficulties with its development, broadcasting issues surrounding wide spread usage and future applications"—Provided by publisher.
  ISBN-13: 978-1-59953-379-7 (library edition : alk. paper)
  ISBN-10: 1-59953-379-0 (library edition : alk. paper)
1. High definition television—Juvenile literature. I. Title.
  TK6679.H576 2010
  384.55—dc22
                                                    2010008699

Manufactured in the United States of America in North Mankato, Minnesota.
164N—072010

Contents

Note: Words that are **bolded** in the text are defined in the glossary on page 44.

Chapter 1

A Sharp Idea

Jonathan will never forget the moment his ideas about TV changed forever. It happened at a friend's house. Jonathan was there to watch a basketball game. When the friend turned on the TV, Jonathan was amazed by the image that appeared. "There were no lines or anything. Just crisp, superb detail. I felt as if I were sitting in the

Spectators watching one of the first available HDTVs in 1998 see the launch of the space shuttle *Discovery*.

stands right then and there," he recalls in his article "Should You Switch to HDTV?" which appeared on Helium.com.

Jonathan had just gotten his first glimpse of **high definition television (HDTV)**. It would not be his last. Jonathan immediately bought an HDTV set of his own. Today he tells anyone who will listen to do the same thing. "It changed the way I want to watch TV," he says.

Jonathan is not the only one who feels this way. Millions of people have bought HDTV sets since 1998, when they first became available to the public. Watchers around the world are now hooked on the high definition experience.

What Is HDTV?

There is a good reason people are getting hooked. HD images are much clearer and

Primary Colors

Red (R), green (G), and blue (B) are known as the primary colors of light. They can combine to create any other color. **Pixels** work on this principle.

Each pixel contains red, green, and blue color bars. Turning off all three color bars makes black. Shining all three bars at top power makes white. Varying the brightness of different bars makes all other shades of color.

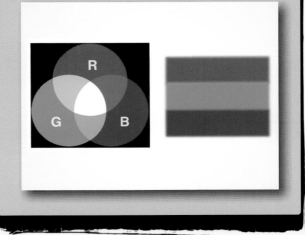

sharper than **standard definition television (SDTV)** pictures. The difference is striking.

HD gets its **clarity** from a feature called resolution. This term describes the amount of visual information in a picture. In simple terms, it counts the number of "chunks" in an image. The more chunks, the better the picture.

On a TV screen, an information chunk is called a pixel. A pixel is a tiny square or rectangle. Each pixel creates one tiny

Resolution

Standard TVs have a resolution of 480i or 480p. High definition TVs have a resolution of 720p, 1080i, or 1080p. This chart shows the number of pixels on each type of screen.

The letters *p* and *i* describe the way screen images are created. On *p* screens, the whole image is shown at once. On *i* screens, only half of the image is shown at any time. The screen flashes the first half, then the second half. It does this over and over. The human eye cannot detect this speedy change. It is fooled into seeing a complete image.

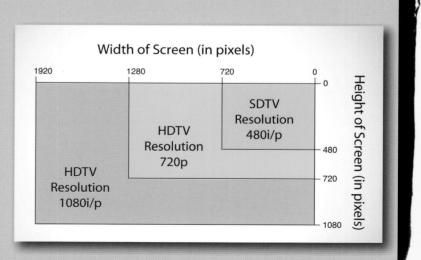

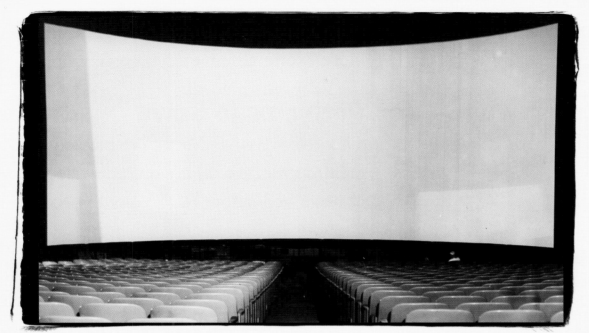

A wide-screen movie theater from 1952 is shown here. Years before HD came to television, movies were being shown in HD on screens like this one.

dot of color. Many pixels combine to form an image on the screen.

The screen of an SDTV has nearly 350,000 pixels. Many HDTV screens have more than two million pixels. More pixels equal higher resolution and a better picture.

Getting the Idea

The idea of better TV images was born at the movies. In the mid-1900s movies were already being shown at high resolutions. TV shows, however, were not. So the difference between home and theater picture resolution was huge.

Did You Know?

The Russian military built an HDTV system called Transformator in 1958. It was never used **commercially**. It was used only by the military.

Movies also had another advantage over TV. They were presented on wide screens. Wider images contained more visual information. This gave viewers more things to look at. Many people thought this made movies more interesting to watch.

Technologists thought they could make TV more like the movies. They could increase the resolution of TV images for movie-like clarity. They could also widen the viewing area. They felt sure that these changes would make TV more exciting than ever before.

Problems to Solve

The idea may have been simple, but the solution was not. Many problems needed to be solved before HDTV could become a reality.

Filming TV shows in HD was the first issue. Regular TV cameras could not capture highly detailed pictures. New high definition cameras and storage methods for film were needed.

Sending the images over the airwaves or via cables was the next challenge. Because HD pictures held so much information, they were "bigger" than SD pictures. They could not be transmitted in the usual ways. Here, too, new methods were required.

Displaying the images on TV sets was the last problem. Standard TVs could not show HD pictures. So TVs with high-definition screens would have to be invented. People would need access to these special TVs to watch HD programs.

Making It Happen

The HDTV challenge was huge but also exciting. Technologists around the world were determined to make it work.

And they did. In 1969 a Japanese company called NHK introduced the world's first commercial HDTV system. The system was called MUSE. It had about four times the resolution of SDTV.

In 1981 NHK demonstrated MUSE at a conference in San Diego, California. The demonstration made a big impact.

In 1935, using a very early version of HD technology, a cameraman shoots footage at a horse-jumping competition.

Using an HD camera, a TV cameraman focuses on the action at a professional golf tournament.

It convinced U.S. broadcasters that they needed HDTV, too. It even impressed then-U.S. president Ronald Reagan. Reagan declared it essential to bring HDTV to the United States.

No one was sure, at that point, that HDTV was practical. Some broadcast-ers decided to find out. Broadcaster Dick Green remembers this "test" period fondly. "Sony agreed to provide two HD cameras and two videotape machines. CBS loaned us an empty truck [to put them into]. We had an all Japanese crew in the truck, running the tape recorders and lining up the cameras and things like that," he recalls in a 2009 interview that appeared on the Multichannel News Web site.

First Green's crew filmed a pro football game. Then they visited the set of a TV series, where they filmed in HD alongside the regular crew. Finally they filmed the Rose Parade in Pasadena, California. "The high-def images of the parade were just stunning," Green remembers.

After three weeks of filming, Green and his crew headed into the editing studio. They made several demo tapes. Then they played the tapes for politicians, broadcasters, and even movie stars. "We showed people it was possible to do *anything* in HD," Green says.

Mission Accomplished

It was possible, yes—but not easy. It took many years for U.S. companies to develop their own HD system. In 1996 they were finally ready. The first American HD signal went out on July 23, 1996. It was sent by WRAL-HD, a station based in Raleigh, North Carolina.

Almost no one saw this broadcast. HDTV sets were not yet available to the

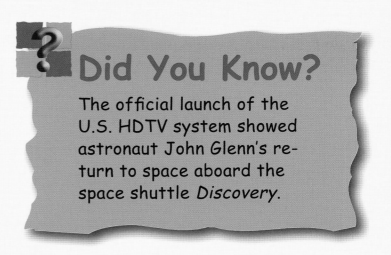

Did You Know?

The official launch of the U.S. HDTV system showed astronaut John Glenn's return to space aboard the space shuttle *Discovery*.

Early models of HDTV sets were expensive. This 61-inch (155cm) model was priced at $7,999.00.

public. But this would soon change. The first HDTVs reached stores in late September 1998. They arrived just in time for the official launch of HDTV over U.S. airwaves on October 29, 1998.

Growing Pains

Anyone with the right TV could now enjoy HDTV. But the technology did not catch on right away. This was partly due to cost. The first HDTV sets were very expensive. Consumers were not convinced that HDTV was worth the money.

Programming was another issue. Broadcasters knew that few HDTV sets were being sold. For this reason, they hesitated to buy HD filming equipment. They did not want to produce HD shows that no one would watch.

Limited programming was a problem even for broadcasters who did buy HD equipment. A station might own just a few HD cameras. It could not use them for every show.

Did You Know?

HD1, Europe's first HD channel, was launched on January 1, 2004.

ESPN vice president Bryan Burns talked about this problem during a 2003 interview that appeared in *HDTV Magazine*'s online edition. "We have one HD truck. That means we can film two to three events a week. We look at things like the NBA [National Basketball Association] finals. Maybe we can do game 2 and game 5, but not if they are farther than 600 miles [966km] apart. We can't get the truck there in time," he said.

Other broadcasters struggled with similar limits. Little by little, though, things got easier. Filming equipment got cheaper, then HD programming increased. At the same time, HDTV sets got cheaper. More and more people bought HDTVs as a result. By the early to mid-2000s an HDTV revolution was under way.

Chapter 2

How It Works

HDTV requires special equipment and techniques. It also involves many steps. It takes a lot of work to produce, transmit, and display high definition TV images.

Getting the Shot

Filming is the first step in HD production. All HDTV pictures are **digital**. This means they are stored as numbers. Broadcasters use special cameras to translate action into this format.

How does it work? HD cameras "see" a scene. Computers inside the cameras break the action into electronic chunks called **bits**. They create more than 1 billion bits per second. These bits create a record of shapes, colors, movement, and other visual cues.

Once a camera creates bits, it stores them. Different cameras have different storage methods. Some HD cameras record onto tape. Others record onto computer discs or hard drives.

The finished recording is stored as a digital file. It does not need to be developed like traditional film. It can be played and watched immediately by anyone with the right computer programs.

This digital video camera, which costs about $50,000, stores both action and sound on a disc.

Sound Effects

Broadcasters capture more than just images when they film. They also capture sound. Microphones record dialogue and other noises during a shoot. These sounds are stored in the same file as the picture information.

In all digital TV, including HDTV, computers split sound files into five or more channels. This system is called surround sound. It sends different parts of a show's soundtrack to different speakers. Voices, for instance, are usually sent to a front speaker. Music might be sent to side and back speakers. Other noises go to speakers that would match their real-life locations.

Viewers can buy surround-sound systems for their homes. These systems in-

A home theater system with surround sound provides vivid sound effects like those in a movie theater.

Did You Know?

Home computers can receive HD images over the Internet. Computer monitors can show them.

clude five speakers (one for each sound channel). Some speakers sit at the front of the viewing area. Others sit to the rear. This arrangement lets sound surround the viewer. The effect can be very exciting. It makes viewers feel like they are part of the action.

Broadcasters took this effect to a new level during the 2009 NBA playoffs. They used a special surround-sound microphone to capture crowd noise in arenas. The crowd noise became part of the broadcast. Home viewers were surrounded by cheering fans, just like they would be at a real arena.

The Squeeze

Raw images and sounds contain huge numbers of bits. This means they create

In 2009, an NBA playoff game filmed using HD and a special microphone lets TV viewers feel as if they are in the middle of the crowd at the game.

very big files. The files are too big for regular broadcast.

To understand why this is the case, imagine a mail carrier. The mail carrier brings information from one place to another. A letter fits into the mail carrier's sack. A big stack of phone books does not. It is much too large.

A satellite dish picks up compressed HD digital files from space to reconfigure them for home TV screens.

Broadcast airwaves and cables are similar to the mail sack. They can only carry a certain amount of information. For this reason, HD files must be "squeezed" to a smaller size before they are sent. This squeeze is called compression.

Compression is done by a computer. During this process the computer removes big chunks of data from a file. It replaces the data with short codes. The codes include instructions for replacing the lost data when the file reaches a TV.

Data compression makes HD files much smaller. The squeezed images are not quite as sharp as the originals. They are, however, much clearer than SD images. Compression is therefore a good compromise. It makes files small enough to send. Yet it keeps most of the clarity that makes HDTV so amazing.

On Its Way

After compression, files are ready for broadcast. HD files may be sent out through cables, over the airwaves, or beamed into space. In space, satellites catch the signals and bounce them back to Earth.

Digital signals of all types eventually reach receivers. Receivers are pieces of

The HDTV Setup

- Airwave or satellite HD signals reach a dish or an antenna (1).
- They travel through cables to a receiver (2), where they are decoded.
- The decoded signal travels through more cables to a monitor (3), where it is displayed.
- Cable signals do not require an antenna or dish. They travel through cables straight to the receiver.

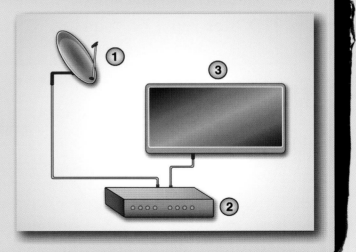

equipment that capture and "read" digital information. They come in many types. Most receivers look like boxes. They are linked to a TV by cables. The receivers send information through these cables.

HDTV sets designed and sold since 2007 have built-in receivers. They can capture airwave signals without any special equipment. They still need receiver boxes for cable or satellite signals, though.

Picture Perfect

Signals are decoded inside an HDTV receiver. The receiver reads the HDTV file as it arrives. It translates bits into image information.

The receiver sends this information to the TV screen. Equipment behind the screen lights up every pixel on the screen, one by one. When every pixel glows, the picture is complete. All of the pixels then

Digital TV and HDTV: Not the Same Thing

Digital TV and HDTV are not the same thing. The term *digital TV* refers to any program recorded as bits. Standard definition shows can be recorded digitally. The term *HDTV* refers to any program recorded at a high resolution. All HD programs are digital, but being digital is not what makes them HD.

turn off. The TV gets to work building a new image.

The screen-lighting process is very fast. HDTVs fill their screens up to 30 times per second. The human brain cannot detect this process. It perceives the individual images, or frames, as moving pictures.

These pictures, of course, come with a soundtrack. HDTV receivers decode sound information along with images. They send this data to the TV's speakers, a viewer's surround-sound system, or both. The sound and the pictures combine to create the HDTV experience.

Did You Know?

Some people put digital antennas on their homes. Digital antennas make airwave signals stronger. This helps them to "catch" weak channels.

The End Result

Very few consumers question HDTV. They do not worry about how it works or where it comes from. They just know they like it. Millions of people enjoy high definition programs every day.

Chapter 3

Living in the HDTV Age

Early HDTVs were very expensive. Many people could not or would not buy them, so sales were slow. But they did happen. Little by little, HDTVs became more common. This caused prices to drop.

Today HDTV sets are more affordable, and an HDTV explosion has been the result. This format is now so popular that it has almost wiped out SDTV in some parts of the world.

This says a lot about the public's viewing habits. People want HDTV. They enjoy life in the high definition age.

Who Watches HDTV?

HDTV is available in many countries. This technology is well established in Japan and Europe as well as in the United States. It is also taking off in Russia. It is spreading more slowly in other areas. But it *is* spreading. Millions

A customer views the many choices available for HDTV sets. As prices have dropped, more people are able to own them.

of new subscribers sign up for HD service every year.

HDTV growth will be spurred by an event called the **digital transition**. This term refers to a change from old-fashioned to digital broadcasting. Many nations still broadcast in **analog** format, which changes information into electronic waves. These nations will eventually switch to the more efficient digital format.

The digital transition is taking place at different times in different places. The United States and some European countries have already made the change. Other nations are still working on it. Soon HDTV will be available everywhere.

The Best Seats in Town

This change will be especially popular with sports fans. Surveys show that the number one reason that people buy HDTVs is to view sporting events.

A 2009 survey proved this fact. More than 1,000 U.S. football fans were asked about their Super Bowl viewing habits. Four out of five people said they would choose HDTV over snacks, if they had to pick.

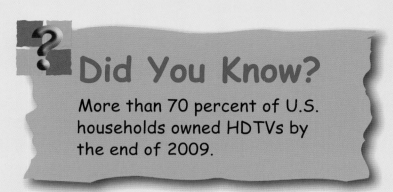

Did You Know?

More than 70 percent of U.S. households owned HDTVs by the end of 2009.

As more people buy HDTVs to watch sports, TV networks have added more events to their sports lineups.

In a *Digital Landing* article entitled "Nothing Finer than Sports in HD," DirectTV spokesman Robert Mercer explains why HD sports are so special. "HD takes you closer to the game. You see the grit on the player's uniform. [You see] beads of sweat on the forehead. If you're not able to sit behind home plate, it's the next best thing."

Sales figures support this statement. In the United States HDTV sales spike every year before the Super Bowl. In Europe the same thing happens before the World Cup soccer tournament. It is clear that sports fans love HDTV.

The Home Theater Experience

Sports may be number one when it comes to HD, but movies are a very close sec-

People can now enjoy the experience of viewing movies in HD on their home theater systems.

ond. Between its sharp pictures and surround sound, HDTV brings the theater experience into viewers' homes.

HD films are especially impressive on large TV sets. The big screen magnifies every detail. It also brings the action up close. Viewers can lose themselves in the story, just like they do in a real theater. In a 2006 review that appeared in the online edition of *High-Def Digest*, writer Peter M. Bracke talked about his reaction to HD home theater. He had been assigned to watch a movie that did not interest him. He also did not like the actor who played the movie's main character. But these things were erased by HD. "Despite the fact that I would normally hate this movie, I loved every single last second of it," he said. "It looked and sounded so good on HD . . . that it actually made me excited to watch [this actor] again. Now, *that* is some kind of technological miracle."

Millions of other viewers feel the same way. Many are ordering HD movies from their cable and satellite providers. Others are buying HD discs and players in stores. People everywhere are making the most of this exciting format.

The Complete Gaming Experience

People are not only buying movies but also games. Gaming systems such as Sony's PlayStation 3 and Microsoft's Xbox 360 hook up to players' HDTVs. They use highly detailed scenes to draw players into the action.

Did You Know?

The 2008 Beijing games were the first Olympics to be filmed and transmitted entirely in HD.

At the 2006 Tokyo Game Show in Japan, a visitor enjoys playing a video game on Sony's PlayStation.

HDTV has made video games far more realistic and exciting. A gamer plays *Call of Duty: Modern Warfare 2* on his XBox system.

Ads show the world how far this technology has come. A trailer for the game *Mirror's Edge,* for example, shows a character's-eye view of a rooftop run. Every detail of the buildings is crystal clear. So are the streets below and the skies above. The character's footsteps and panting breath stand out against quieter background noises. Viewers feel like they are seeing with the character's eyes and hearing with her ears.

In the comments section following a 1up.com article entitled "Mark Rein: Emphasis on HD Gaming Is Overrated," one gamer describes his very different feelings about HDTV: "[It] has changed the way I look at games. I bought more than 15 games for my [HD system] last year. That's more than I bought during the entire lifetime [of my old SD system]. With HD, I just wanna play and play and play."

All or Nothing

HDTV pictures never get snowy or fuzzy. They are either crystal clear or nonexistent. This is because digital signals are so simple. They are just long strings of numbers. If a receiver can make out these numbers, the picture is perfect. If it cannot read the numbers, the screen goes blank. Broadcasters call this the cliff effect.

Old Favorites, New Quality

Sports, movies, and games are the biggest HDTV draws. But regular programs are catching up. People can see most of their favorite shows in HD.

It might not seem like this should be a huge deal. A show has the same characters and plot at any resolution. But it turns out that HDTV *is* a big deal. Crime-ridden streets seem grittier. Comedians' facial expressions are funnier. Characters seem more real. These changes make network TV shows more enjoyable for viewers.

Music and awards programs are especially popular in HD. During the Oscars or other events, viewers can see every sparkling sequin on each gown. They can see the lint on the red carpet. These details make the events more vivid. Viewers feel like they are part of the scene.

Changing Perceptions

HDTV does not just make shows more enjoyable. It can provide extra visual information, too. This in turn can change the way people think and feel about things.

The 2007 documentary series *Planet Earth* had this effect. This series was filmed entirely in HD. It showed the Earth's animals and remote places with never-before-seen clarity. By doing this, it helped people to experience the Earth in new ways.

One woman described this feeling in an online review. "Our whole family was in awe. . . . After you watch this show, I guarantee you will have a whole new appreciation and outlook for our wondrous, beautiful planet," she says.

Cleaning Up Their Act

Every detail shows up clearly in HD. This fact has forced broadcasters to clean up their act—literally! Today's sets, lighting, and camera angles must be perfect. The smallest defect will be noticeable to viewers.

The same is true for people. One TV critic remembers watching a movie star on the red carpet. In SD the woman's skin looked perfect. Yet in HD pimples were visible across the star's forehead. Makeup artists have learned how to deal with situations like this. They have developed products and techniques that make their clients look great in HD.

A makeup artist applies special makeup to a model before she is filmed in HD.

Worldwide HDTV

In some ways HDTV is helping to create a global community. Broadcasters in many nations now produce HD programs. Satellites beam these programs all over the world. People everywhere can watch the broadcasts. For the first time, they can experience other countries and cultures in high definition.

Many other viewers feel the same way. They have urged their friends to buy the series—but only in an HD format. "Watching this under anything less than high definition doesn't do [it] justice," says one happy reviewer on Amazon.com. This person enjoys the benefits of HD. He wants others to have the same experience.

Changing the World

All TVs bring new sights, sounds, and experiences into people's homes. They are like windows to the world. HDTV enhances this experience by making the window bigger and clearer. It helps people to see things in new ways. This is one of many reasons why HDTV is now a "must-have" for viewers everywhere.

Chapter 4

Changing the Way We Watch

HDTV has already had a huge impact on the world. The HD revolution, however, is far from over. Technologists around the world are working to make HDTV even better. They are also changing old technologies to make them more useful with HDTV. Today's advances will continue to change the way people watch and use their TVs.

Bigger Is Better

Bigger TVs may be the most obvious effect of the HD switch. HDTVs seem to get larger every year. At the end of 2009, electronics stores sold HDTVs measuring up to 70 inches (178cm) diagonally.

TVs are growing in size for a very good reason. Digital images look even sharper as they grow. This fact adds to HDTV's appeal.

Gigantic HDTVs, like this one hanging above a soccer game being played at the Dallas Cowboys football stadium, give fans a chance to view themselves in HD.

Big TVs have changed the look of people's homes. "I bought a 53-inch [135cm] HDTV. It is in the living room of my 100-year-old Victorian home. The furniture is arranged to provide the best possible viewing and to take full advantage of the surround sound," says one woman in the HDTV Info Port article "HDTV: A Woman's View." "My husband wanted a smaller set. But when it comes to HDTV, size does matter. And I wanted every inch I could get." The size/distance ratio is important when watching a large-screen TV.

HD Billboards

Many businesses feel the same way. They have used HD technology to create giant public displays. They hope these displays will attract attention in a way that SD does not.

Two big displays are found in New York City's Times Square. The largest one is owned by Walgreens. It towers 340 feet (104m) above ground level. It has thirteen separate screens. A smaller display is run by electronics company JVC. It measures 19 by 34 feet (6 by 10m). It hangs just one story above ground level, where it is guaranteed to be seen.

Did You Know?

Many newer computers have built-in HD disc drives.

A stack of massive HD "billboards" towers above Times Square in New York City.

Some people love these HD billboards. Others think they are too flashy. But *everyone* notices them. "It's amazing to travel to New York and see these amazing displays lighting up an otherwise drab-looking building," says one man in the 2008 *New York Times* article "LEDs Light Jumbo Sign in Times Square."

Make Way for Blu-ray

In the HDTV age, bigger is also better when it comes to data storage. HD files require lots of digital memory. High-capacity discs meet this need.

Blu-ray is the most common format. Blu-ray discs are the same size and

Almosts: HD DVD

Blu-ray discs are now the standard high-capacity storage system. But they had to beat out a competitor to get there.

A format called HD DVD was introduced around the same time as Blu-ray. It was available for two years. During this time about one million HD DVD players were sold. This number was not good enough, however, to conquer Blu-ray. In early 2008 manufacturers announced that they would stop making HD DVDs. This decision allowed Blu-ray to take control of the market.

shape as CDs and DVDs. But they carry much more information. One Blu-ray disc can hold almost 40 times more data than a CD. It can hold over five times more data than a DVD. This means it can contain a high definition film—something a regular DVD could not do.

Most films are now available on Blu-ray. To watch, a viewer puts the disc into a special Blu-ray player. The player reads the disc. It sends sound and picture information to the viewer's HDTV. Then the movie is shown at the highest possible resolution.

HD in 3-D

Soon viewers may be able to watch their favorite movies in three dimensions as

Another innovation for home theaters will be 3-D HDTV. A Panasonic model plays the 3-D movie *Avatar* at a Las Vegas trade show.

well. Three-dimensional films create the illusion of depth. People and objects seem to "pop" off the screen.

By 2010, 3-D movies were very popular in theaters. Manufacturers hoped to copy this success with 3-D HDTV shows.

The first step in this process is already done. Samsung, Mitsubishi, and other companies launched 3-D HDTV models in 2008. These televisions come with special glasses. Viewers wear the glasses to see shows in high definition 3-D.

Analysts think 3-D HDTVs will be very popular. They point to the success of 3-D films as proof. "Consumers are voting with their wallets today for the 3-D version of their favorite movie in the theater," says one HDTV expert in the 2009 article "3DTV Shipments Set to Reach 46 Million by 2013, According to GigaOm Pro." "Many will choose 3-D for their favorite shows and movies at home as well."

As Clear as the Real Thing

These programs may look even better than today's HD shows thanks to another development. A Japanese company is working on higher-resolution HDTVs.

A consumer wears special glasses to try out a 3-D video game at a 2010 trade show.

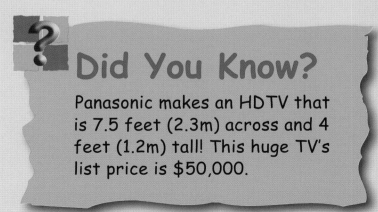

Did You Know?

Panasonic makes an HDTV that is 7.5 feet (2.3m) across and 4 feet (1.2m) tall! This huge TV's list price is $50,000.

Record Breaker

The world's largest HDTV set was unveiled in 2008. Built by the Matsushita Company, the enormous TV measures 150 inches (381cm) diagonally. The display area is about 11.5 feet (3.5m) wide and 6.5 feet (2m) tall. Consumers are not likely to buy a TV this big. But that is not really the point, says market researcher Eric Haruki. Haruki believes that these large TVs could be used as billboards by companies. Making incredibly large TVs also shows off the maker's technical abilities.

A person is dwarfed by the Japanese-built Panasonic 150-inch (381cm) HD plasma TV screen, the world's largest.

The new format is called **Super Hi-Vision**.

Super Hi-Vision screens contain about sixteen times more information than to-day's best HD screens. This level of detail is incredibly vivid. In test screenings many viewers tried to touch the TV screen. They wanted to see if the images were real.

It will be many years before Super Hi-Vision reaches the public. But it is coming. The Japanese government is starting a group to work on this format. It hopes to launch Super Hi-Vision in the year 2020.

HDTV on the Job

Super Hi-Vision may be far off, but other exciting developments are already here.

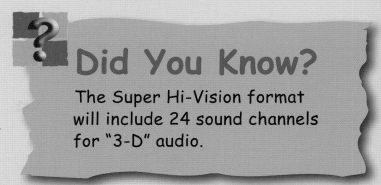

Did You Know?

The Super Hi-Vision format will include 24 sound channels for "3-D" audio.

People in every profession are finding new ways to use HDTV.

Law enforcement is one of these professions. Some **surveillance** systems now use HD cameras and monitors. HD night-vision goggles are also available. These tools give officers a better view of their surroundings. They make it easier and safer for the officers to do their jobs.

Doctors are finding uses for HD technology, too. One exciting change involves instruments called endoscopes. These are

Using HD technology, the tiny endoscope allows doctors to view the insides of their patients' bodies.

tiny cameras that a doctor inserts into a patient's body to look for diseased tissue or other problems.

Some doctors are now using HD endoscopes and monitors. These tools help doctors to see better inside a patient's body. As a result, they can make better diagnoses. They can also be more precise during surgeries.

Police officers and doctors are not the only ones using HDTV. Other professionals are adopting it, too. Airline pilots, office workers, commercial divers, and many other workers are using this technology.

Children watch an HD image of a polar bear at a zoo in Tokyo. Well-placed cameras allow zoo visitors vivid HD views of the exhibits.

They are seeing firsthand how HDTV can make their lives easier.

What Next?

Any technology can be improved in endless ways. Television is no exception. HDTV may be amazing, but it is just a glimpse of things yet to come. Super Hi-Vision, 3-D HDTV, and other inventions will continue to revolutionize the TV experience. In doing so, they will make a great idea even better.

Glossary

analog: Recorded and transmitted as a continuous electronic wave. Changes in the wave's shape and strength translate into sound and image information.

bits: The smallest elements of computer storage. Bits can have a value of either 1 or 0.

Blu-ray: A high-capacity digital storage format.

clarity: The quality of being clear; sharply focused.

commercially: In a manner available to the general public.

compression: A process that removes unneeded information from digital files to make them smaller and easier to send.

digital: Recorded and transmitted as a series of bits.

digital transition: The switch from analog to digital broadcasting.

high definition television (HDTV): A television that displays images at a higher resolution than standard TVs.

pixels: Single visual units on a TV screen. Each pixel contains one red, one green, and one blue bar.

standard definition television (SDTV): A television format that cannot display HD. Compared to HDTV, its picture is less crisp and shows less detail.

Super Hi-Vision: An experimental format that contains sixteen times more visual information than current HDTV systems.

surveillance: Keeping close watch on a person or group, especially where illegal activity is suspected.

technologists: Specialists who are trained in various fields of technology.

For More Information

Web Sites to Visit

CNET (www.cnet.com/hdtv-world). This Web site includes the section "HDTV World," which covers every aspect of HDTV, from buying to using and everything in between.

HDTV Infoport (www.hdtvinfoport.com/ HDTV.html). This Web site, which includes the article "HDTV—Demystified," explains HDTV basics, such as what the parts are called and what various abbreviations mean.

HowStuffWorks (www.howstuffworks .com/hdtv.htm). This Web site offers a slightly more advanced explanation of how HDTV works. It includes many good pictures.

"Spectrum Wars" (www.nationaljournal .com/scripts/printpage.cgi?/about/nj weekly/stories/2005/0218njsp.htm). This article, written by Drew Clark of *Technology Daily*, explains the politics behind HDTV's U.S. launch.

Index

A
Analog format, 23
Antennas, 21

B
Billboards, 35–36, 40
Bits, 14, 17
Blu-ray, 36–37
Bracke, Peter M., 26
Broadcast/broadcasters,
    10–11, 19–20, 31
Burns, Bryan, 13

C
Cameras, HD, 8, 13, 41
    workings of, 14–15
Cliff effect, 29

D
Digital Landing (magazine),
    25

Digital pictures, 14
Digital transition, 23–24
Digital TV, 20
Discs, Blu-ray, 36–37

E
Endoscope, 41–42

G
Gaming systems, 26, 29
GigaOm Pro, 39
Glenn, John, 11
Green, Dick, 10–11

H
HD DVD, 37
HDTV Magazine, 13
HDTV sets, 12–13, 22
    size of, 33, 34, 39, 40
High-Def Digest (magazine),
    26

High definition television
    (HDTV), 5–6
    advances in, 39, 41, 43
    digital TV *vs.,* 20
    first U.S. launch of,
        11–12
    idea of, 7–8
    on-the-job use of, 41–42
    setup for, 19
    for sports shows, 24–25
    worldwide use of, 24, 32

L
Law enforcement, 41

M
Medical technology, 41–42
Mercer, Robert, 25
Movies, 7–8, 25–26
    in 3-D, 37–38
MUSE system, 9–10

About the Author

Kris Hirschmann has written more than 200 books for children. She lives just outside Orlando, Florida with her husband, Michael, and her daughters, Nikki and Erika. She has owned an HDTV since 2003, and she enjoys watching movies in HD with her family.